HAL•LEONARD®
BASS
PLAY-ALONG

AUDIO
ACCESS
INCLUDED

PAUL McCARTNEY

VOL. 43

PLAYBACK+
Speed • Pitch • Balance • Loop

To access audio visit:
www.halleonard.com/mylibrary

Enter Code
7693-8045-5094-0471

Cover photo courtesy of MPL Communications

ISBN 978-1-4584-2361-0

HAL•LEONARD®

Visit Hal Leonard Online at
www.halleonard.com

Contact Us:
Hal Leonard
7777 West Bluemound Road
Milwaukee, WI 53213
Email: info@halleonard.com

In Europe contact:
Hal Leonard Europe Limited
Distribution Centre, Newmarket Road
Bury St Edmunds, Suffolk, IP33 3YB
Email: info@halleonardeurope.com

In Australia contact:
Hal Leonard Australia Pty. Ltd.
4 Lentara Court
Cheltenham, Victoria, 3192 Australia
Email: info@halleonard.com.au

Page	Title
6	Band on the Run
22	Hey Bulldog
30	I Want You (She's So Heavy)
17	Live and Let Die
44	Maybe I'm Amazed
51	Penny Lane
60	Rain
76	Silly Love Songs
68	With a Little Help from My Friends

BASS NOTATION LEGEND

Bass music can be notated two different ways: on a *musical staff,* and in *tablature*

Notes:

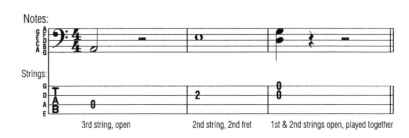

Strings:

THE MUSICAL STAFF shows pitches and rhythms and is divided by bar lines into measures. Pitches are named after the first seven letters of the alphabet.

TABLATURE graphically represents the bass fingerboard. Each horizontal line represents a string, and each number represents a fret.

3rd string, open   2nd string, 2nd fret   1st & 2nd strings open, played together

HAMMER-ON: Strike the first (lower) note with one finger, then sound the higher note (on the same string) with another finger by fretting it without picking.

PULL-OFF: Place both fingers on the notes to be sounded. Strike the first note and without picking, pull the finger off to sound the second (lower) note.

LEGATO SLIDE: Strike the first note and then slide the same fret-hand finger up or down to the second note. The second note is not struck.

SHIFT SLIDE: Same as legato slide, except the second note is struck.

TRILL: Very rapidly alternate between the notes indicated by continuously hammering on and pulling off.

TREMOLO PICKING: The note is picked as rapidly and continuously as possible.

VIBRATO: The string is vibrated by rapidly bending and releasing the note with the fretting hand.

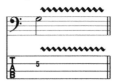

SHAKE: Using one finger, rapidly alternate between two notes on one string by sliding either a half-step above or below.

NATURAL HARMONIC: Strike the note while the fret hand lightly touches the string directly over the fret indicated.

MUFFLED STRINGS: A percussive sound is produced by laying the fret hand across the string(s) without depressing them and striking them with the pick hand.

BEND: Strike the note and bend up the interval shown.

BEND AND RELEASE: Strike the note and bend up as indicated, then release back to the original note. Only the first note is struck.

RIGHT-HAND TAP: Hammer ("tap") the fret indicated with the "pick-hand" index or middle finger and pull off to the note fretted by the fret hand.

LEFT-HAND TAP: Hammer ("tap") the fret indicated with the "fret-hand" index or middle finger.

SLAP: Strike ("slap") string with right-hand thumb.

POP: Snap ("pop") string with right-hand index or middle finger.

Additional Musical Definitions

(accent) • Accentuate note (play it louder)

(accent) • Accentuate note with great intensity

(staccato) • Play the note short

D.S. al Coda • Go back to the sign (𝄋), then play until the measure marked ***"To Coda"***, then skip to the section labelled ***"Coda."***

Fill • Label used to identify a brief pattern which is to be inserted into the arrangement.

 • Repeat measures between signs.

 • When a repeated section has different endings, play the first ending only the first time and the second ending only the second time.

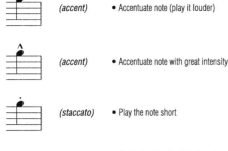

Band on the Run

Words and Music by Paul McCartney and Linda McCartney

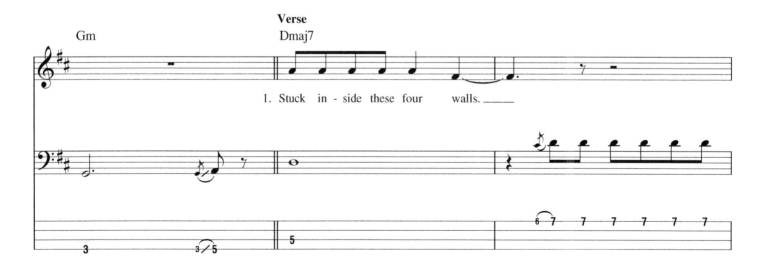

1. Stuck in - side these four walls. _____

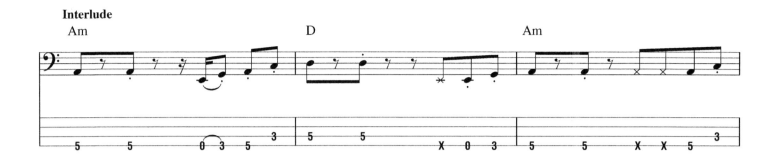

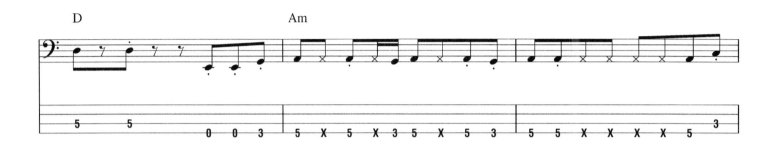

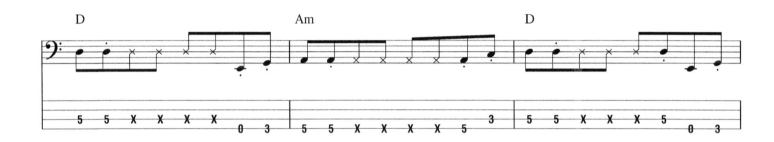

Bridge

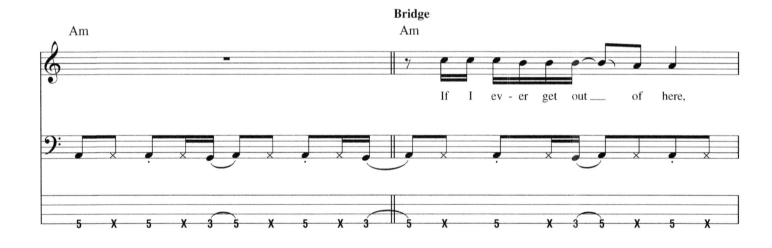

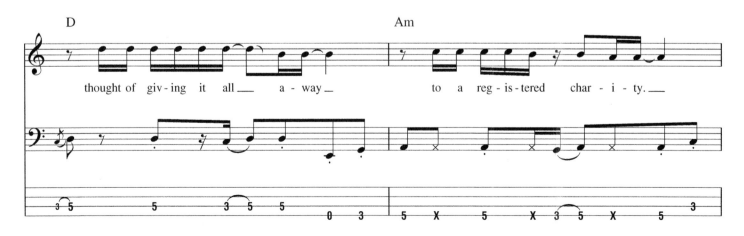

If I ev-er get out ___ of here,

thought of giv-ing it all ___ a-way ___ to a reg-is-tered char-i-ty. ___

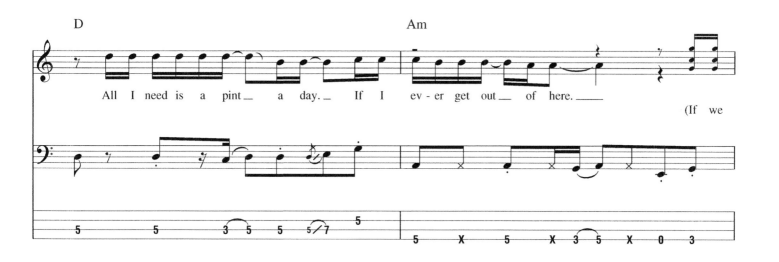

All I need is a pint a day. If I ev-er get out of here. (If we

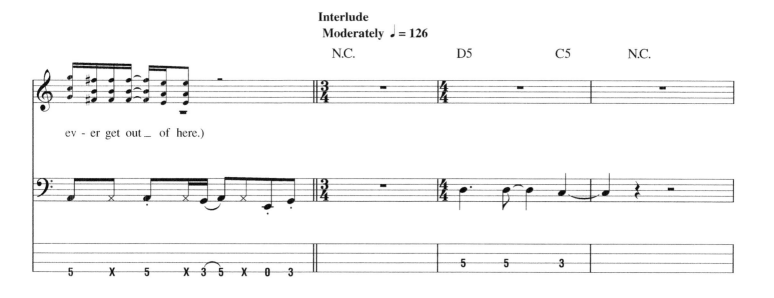

Interlude
Moderately ♩ = 126

ev-er get out of here.)

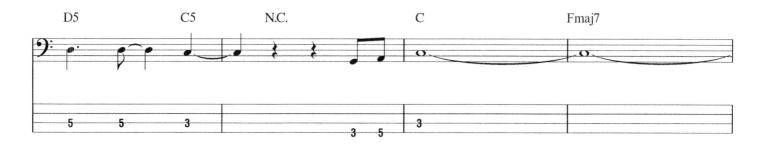

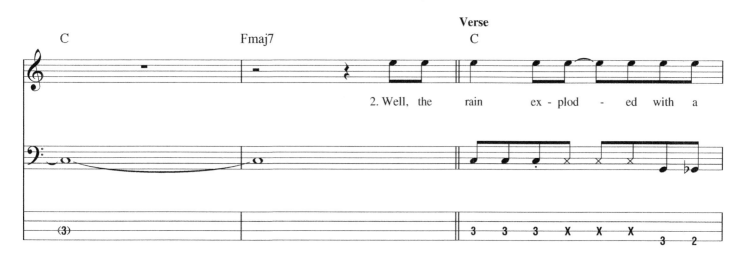

Verse

2. Well, the rain ex-plod-ed with a

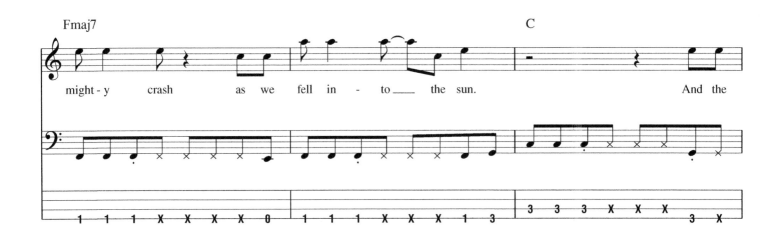

might-y crash as we fell in-to ___ the sun. And the

first one said to the sec-ond one there, ___ "I hope you're hav - ing fun." ___

Pre-Chorus

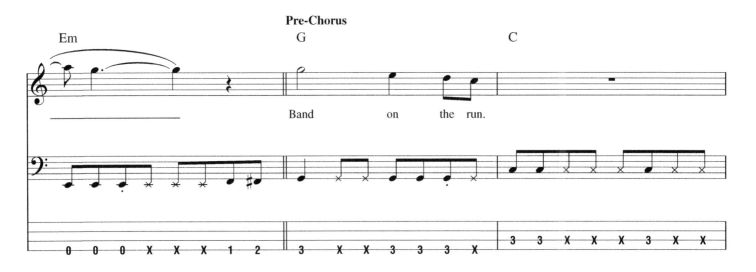

___ Band on the run.

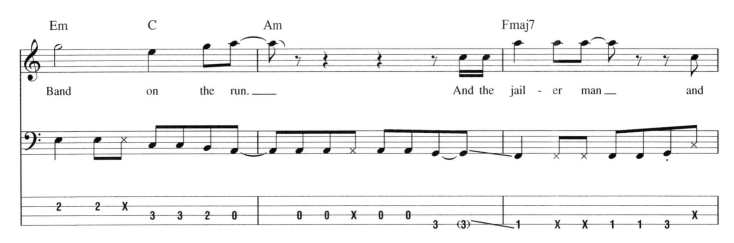

Band on the run. ___ And the jail - er man ___ and

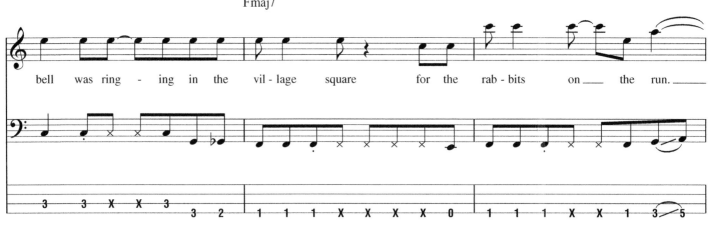

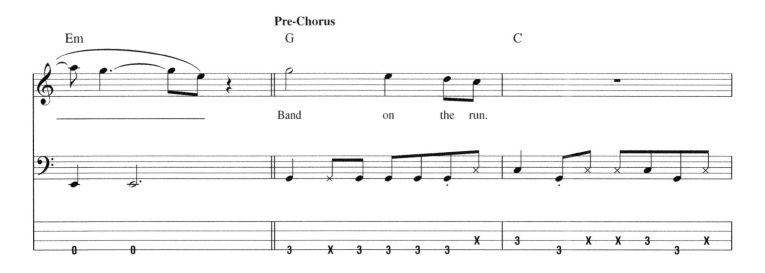

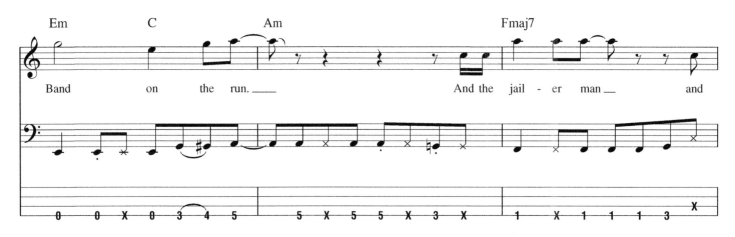

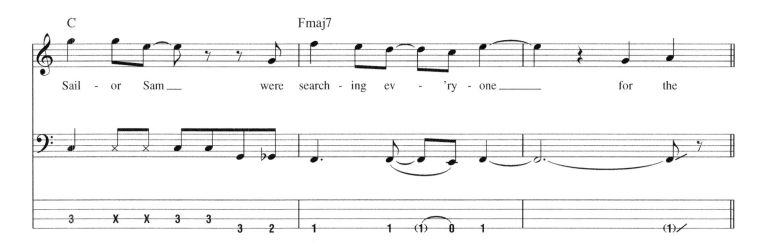

Sail - or Sam___ were search - ing ev - 'ry - one____ for the

Chorus

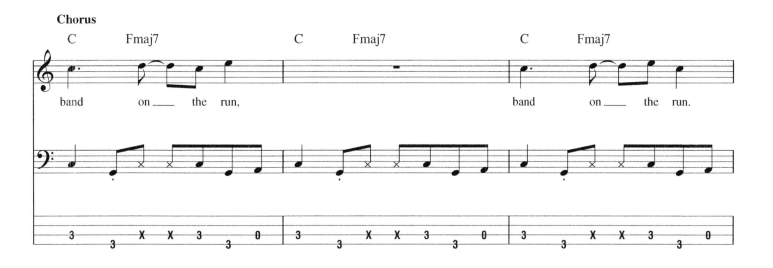

band on ___ the run, band on ___ the run.

Interlude

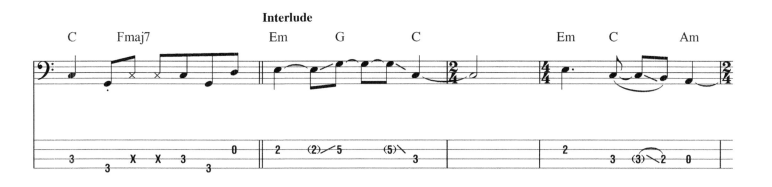

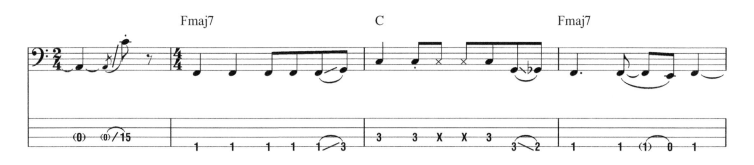

Chorus

Yeah, the band on the run, the
band on the run. Band on the run,
yeah, band on the run. 4. Well, the

Verse

night was fall - ing as the des - ert world began to set - tle down.

steady gliss.

Live and Let Die

Words and Music by Paul McCartney and Linda McCartney

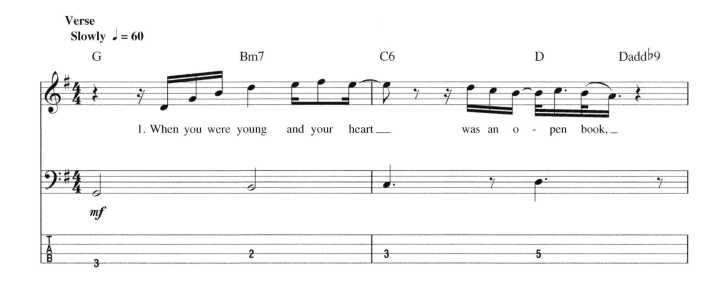

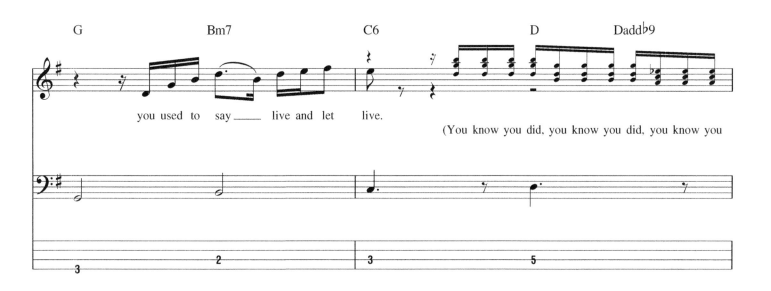

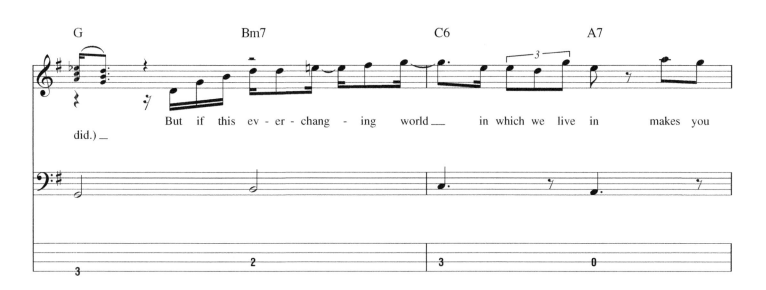

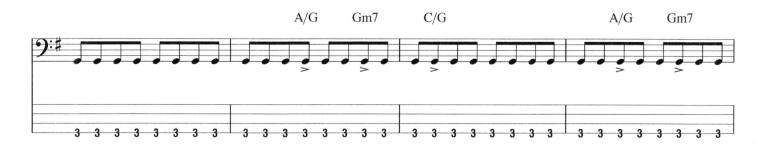

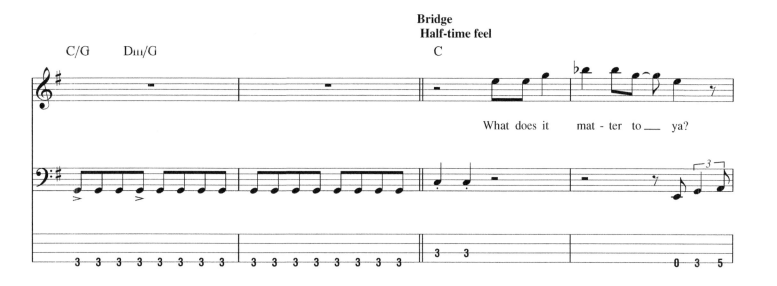

Bridge
Half-time feel

What does it mat - ter to ___ ya?

When you got a job to do, ___ you got - ta do it well. ___ You got to

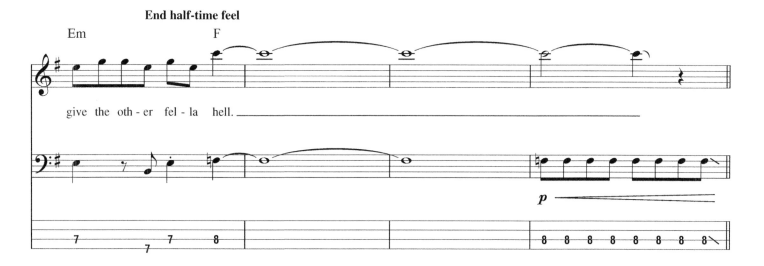

End half-time feel

give the oth - er fel - la hell. ___

Interlude

N.C.(Gm7)

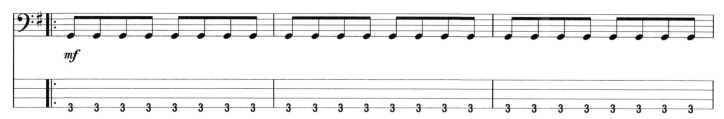

Tempo I

G　　Bm7　　C6　　D　Dadd♭9

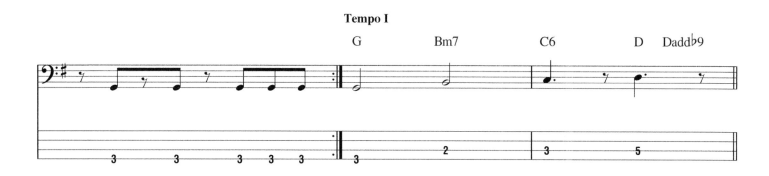

Verse

G　　Bm7　　C6　　D　Dadd♭9

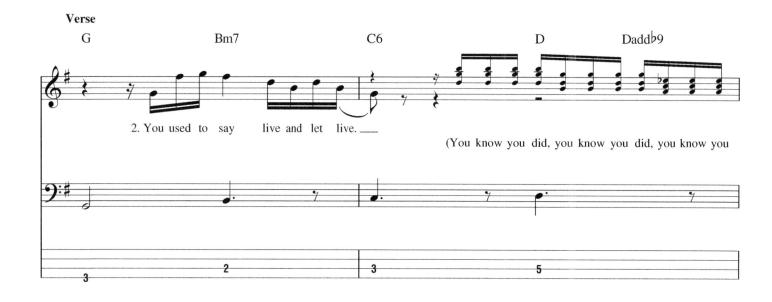

2. You used to say　live and let live. ___

(You know you did, you know you did, you know you

G　　Bm7　　C6　　A7

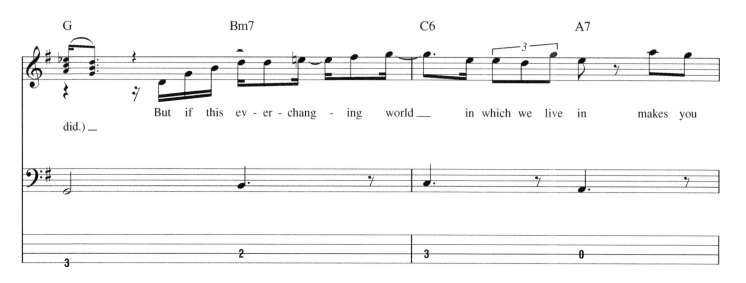

But if this ev - er - chang - ing world ___ in which we live in makes you

did.) ___

give in and cry, ___ say live and let die. ___

(Live and let

die. ___ Live and let die. ___ Live and let die.) ___

Outro
Tempo II

N.C.(Gm7)

Play 3 times

E♭m

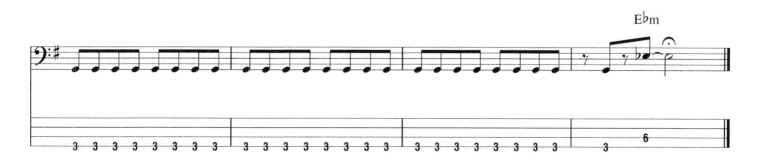

Hey Bulldog

Words and Music by John Lennon and Paul McCartney

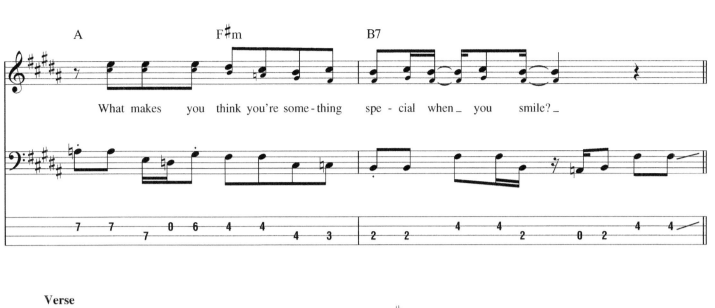

What makes you think you're some-thing spe - cial when_ you smile?_

Verse

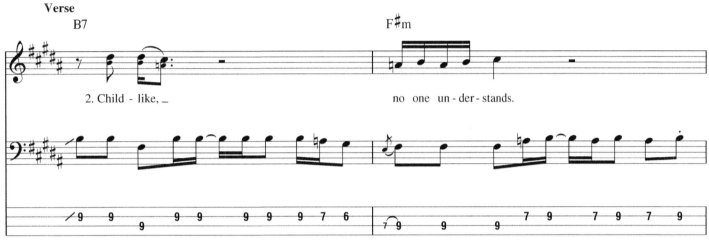

2. Child - like, _ no one un - der - stands.

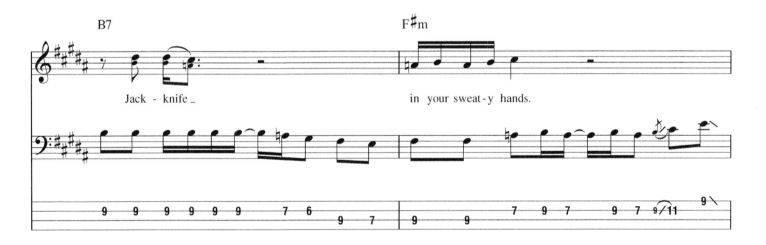

Jack - knife _ in your sweat - y hands.

Some kind of in - no - cence _ is meas - ured out _ in years. _

You don't know what it's like ___ to lis-ten to ___ your fears. ___

Chorus

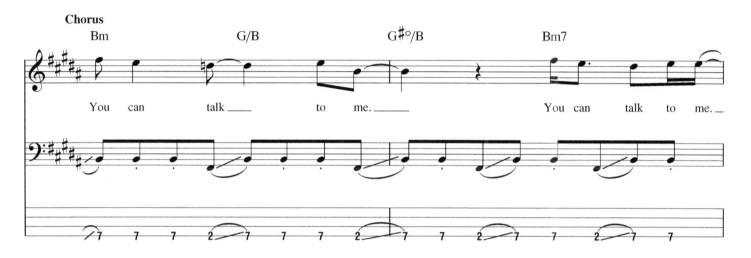

You can talk ___ to me. ___ You can talk to me. ___

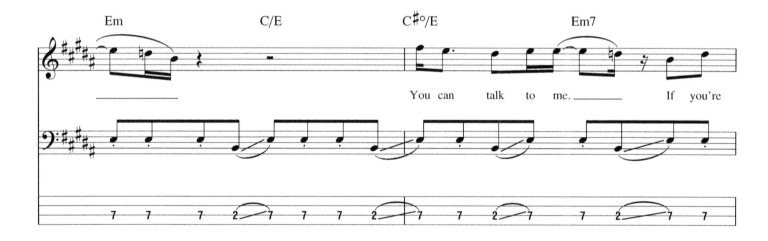

You can talk to me. ___ If you're

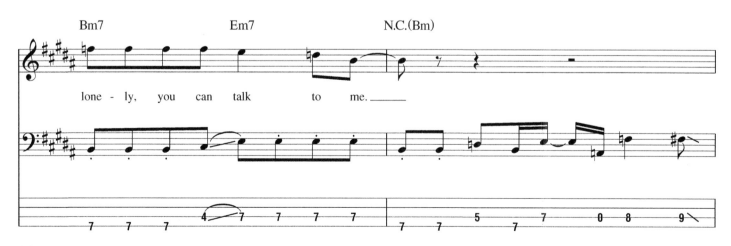

lone-ly, you can talk to me. ___

Guitar Solo

B7

F#m
B7

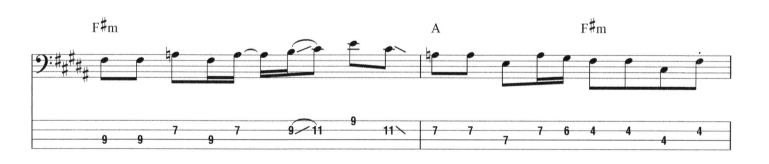

F#m
A
F#m

E
E/D
A
F#m

Outro

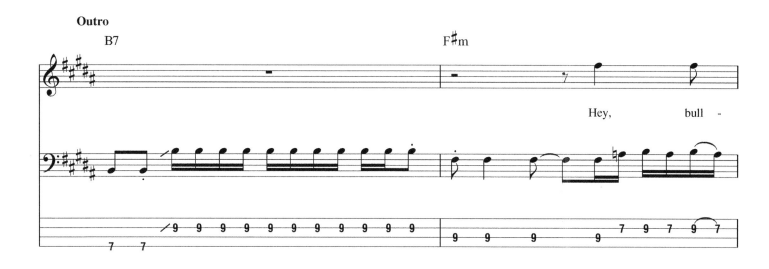

Hey, bull -

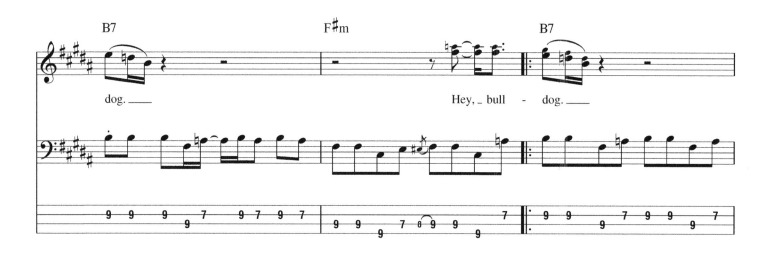

dog. _____ Hey, _ bull - dog. _____

Hey, _____ bull - dog. _____

I Want You
(She's So Heavy)

Words and Music by John Lennon and Paul McCartney

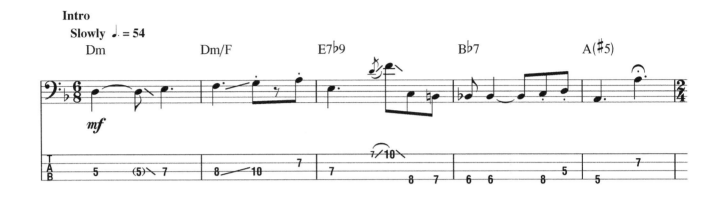

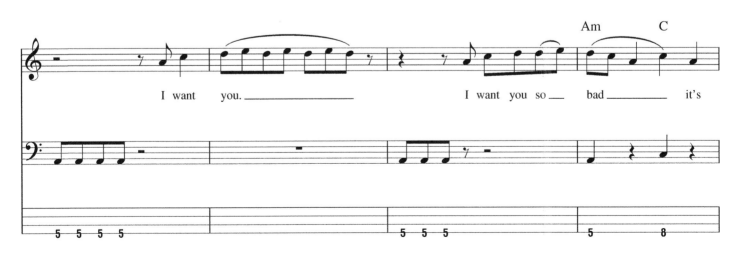

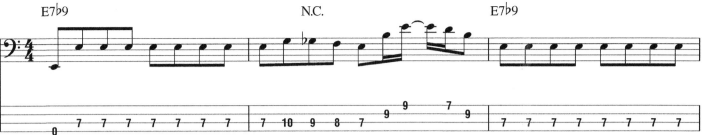

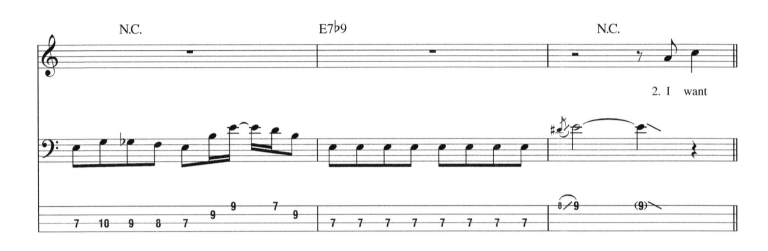

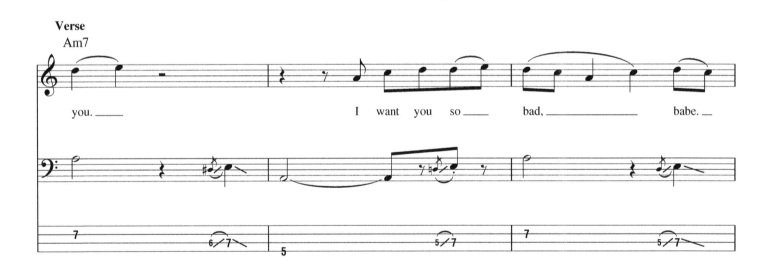

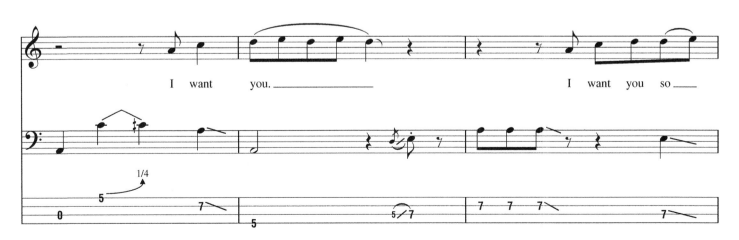

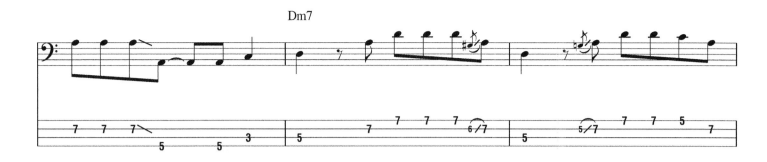

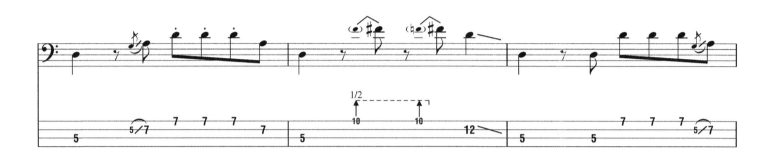

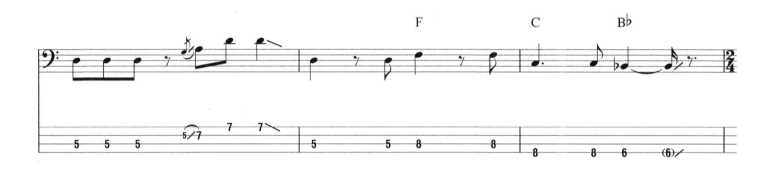

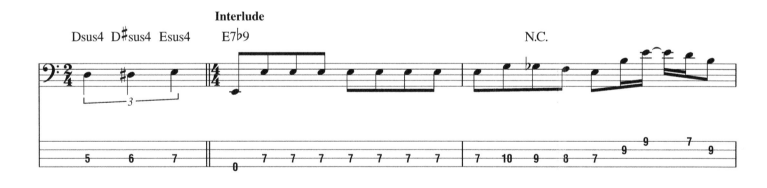

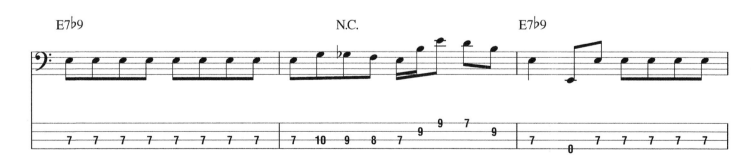

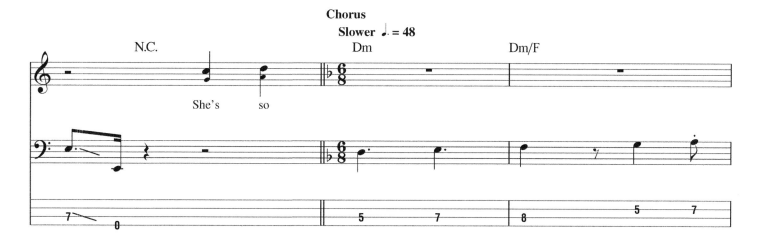

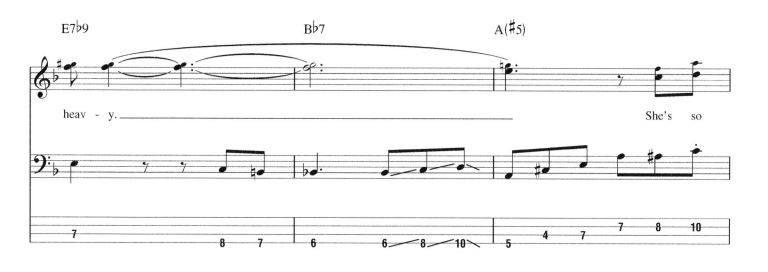

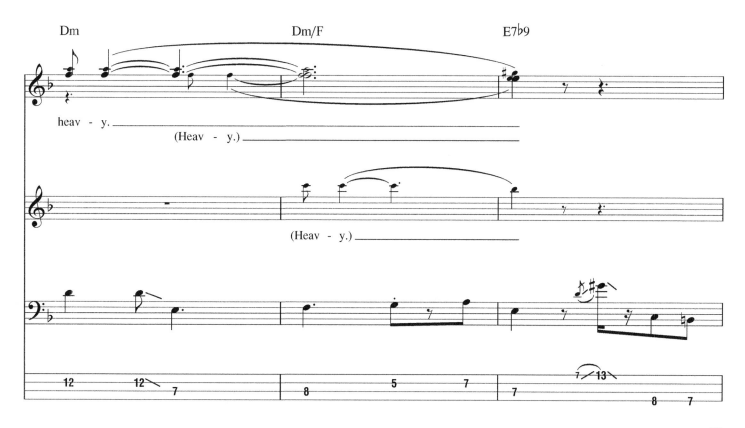

Maybe I'm Amazed

Words and Music by Paul McCartney

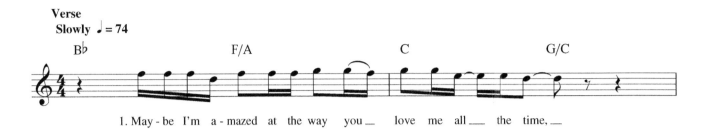

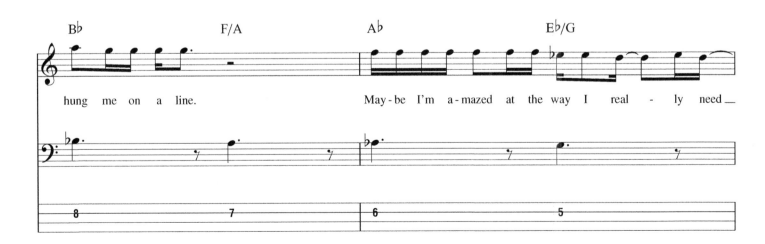

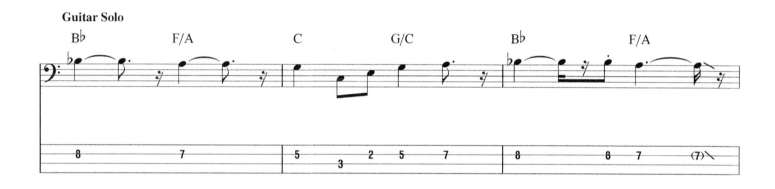

Guitar Solo

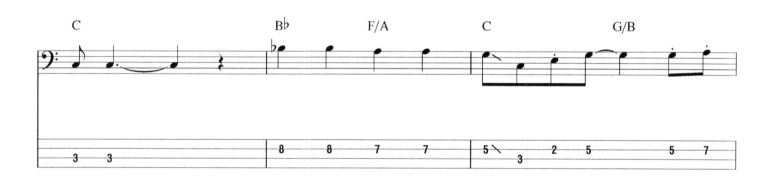

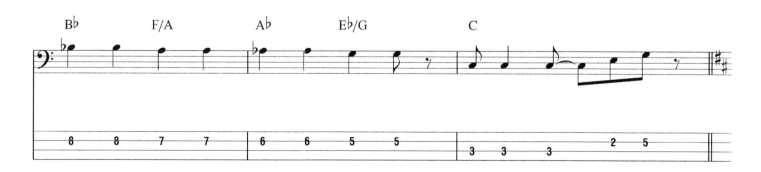

Outro-Guitar Solo
A tempo

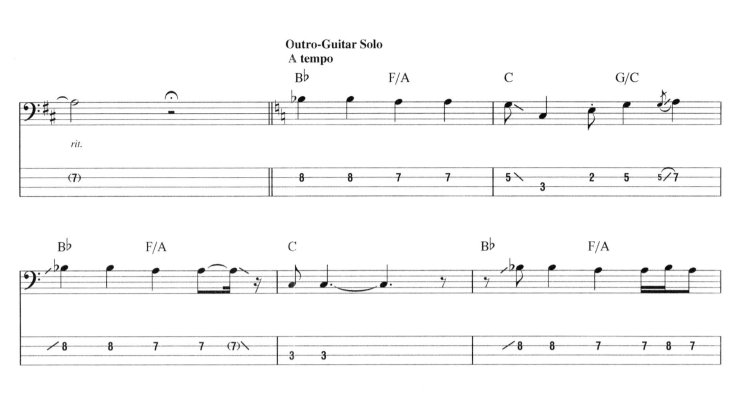

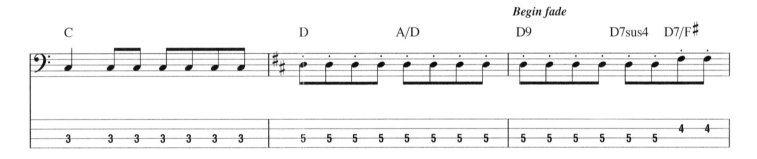

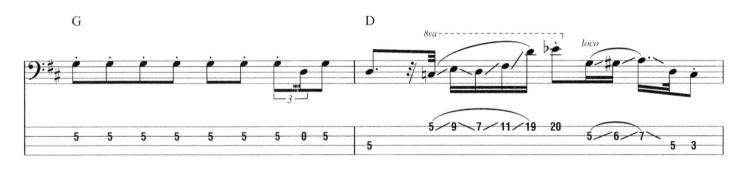

Penny Lane

Words and Music by John Lennon and Paul McCartney

1. Pen - ny Lane, _____ there is a bar - ber show - ing pho -

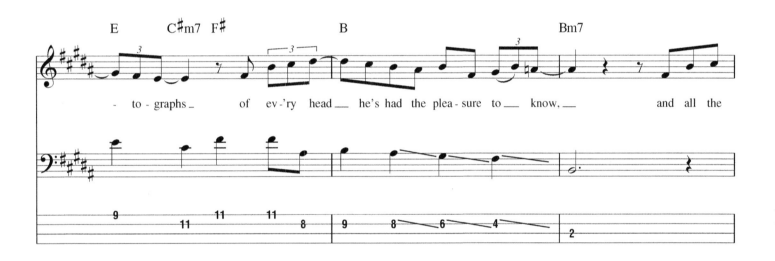

- to - graphs _ of ev'ry head _ he's had the plea - sure to _ know, _ and all the

peo - ple that come and go, _____ stop and say _ hel - lo. _____ 2. On the

Verse

cor - ner is a bank - er with a mo - tor car.___ The lit - tle chil -

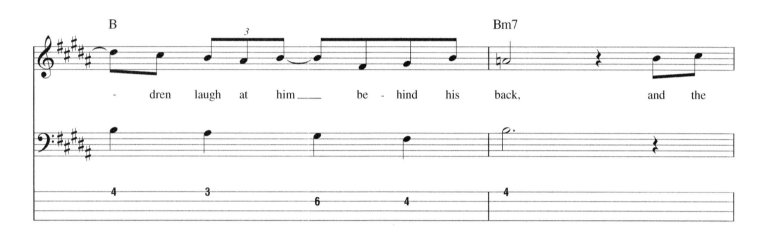

- dren laugh at him___ be - hind his back, and the

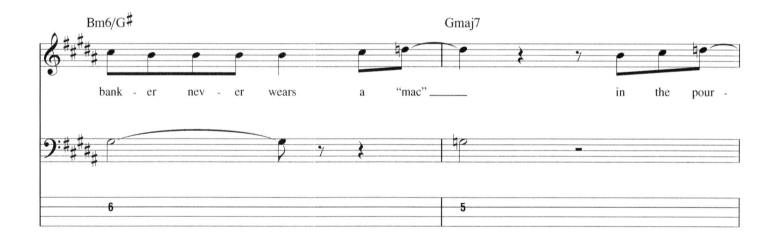

bank - er nev - er wears a "mac" _____ in the pour -

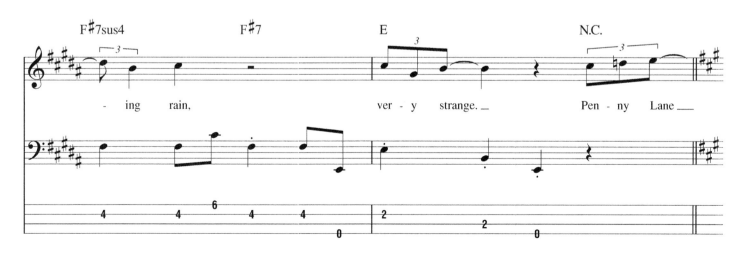

- ing rain, ver - y strange.___ Pen - ny Lane ___

- et is a por - trait of the Queen. He likes to

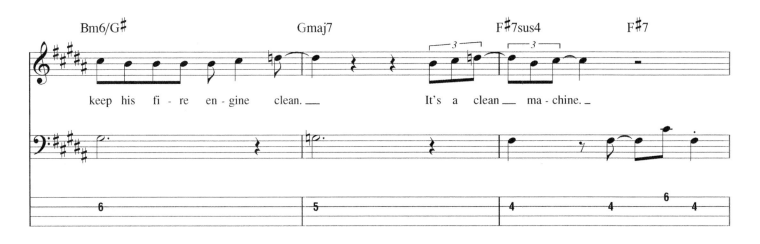

Bm6/G♯   Gmaj7   F♯7sus4   F♯7

keep his fi - re en - gine clean. It's a clean ma - chine.

Piccolo Trumpet Solo

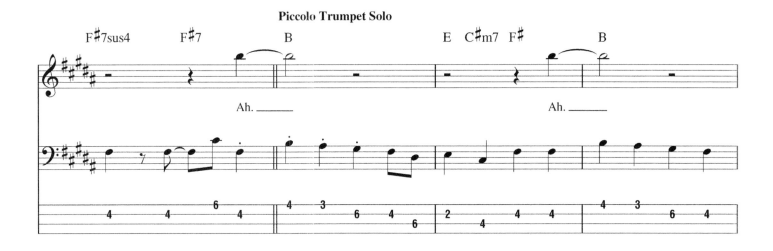

F♯7sus4   F♯7   B   E C♯m7 F♯   B

Ah.   Ah.

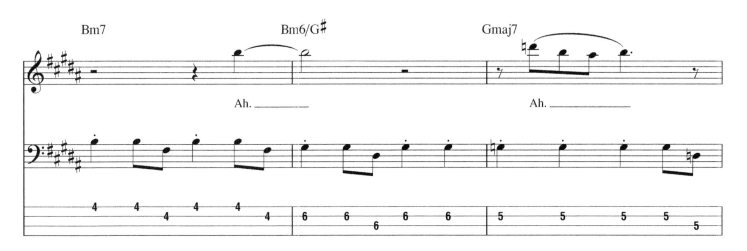

Bm7   Bm6/G♯   Gmaj7

Ah.   Ah.

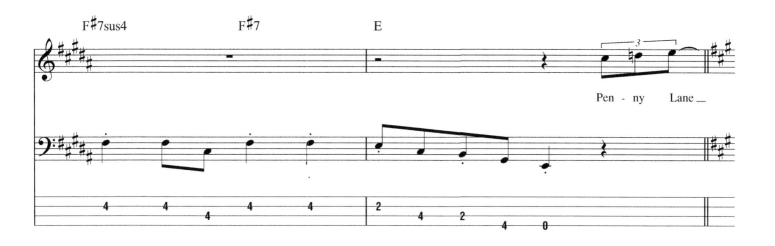

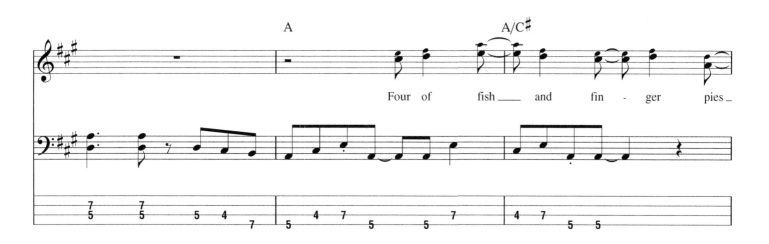

Chorus

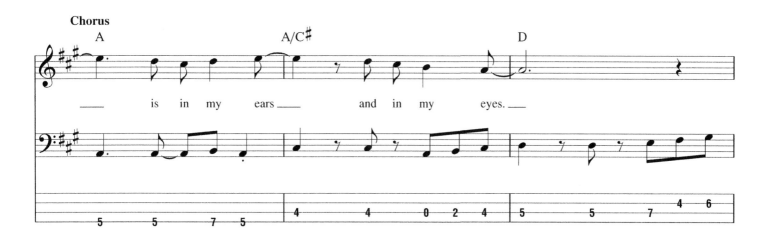

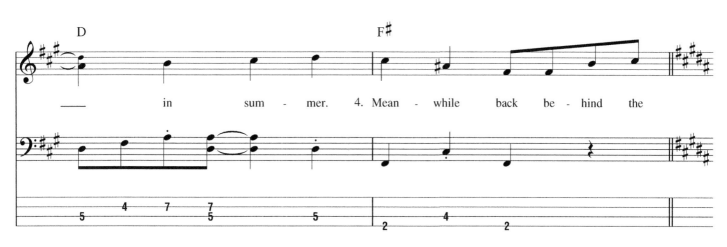

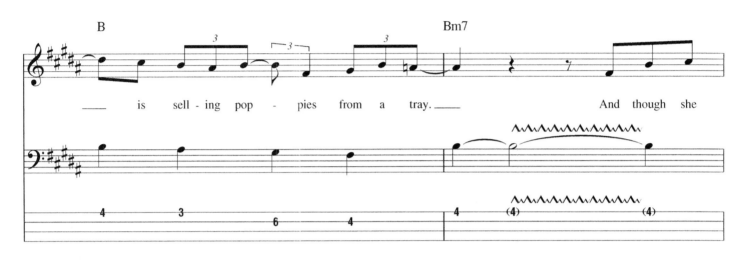

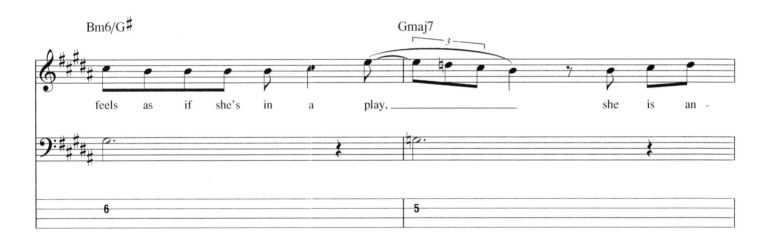

Verse

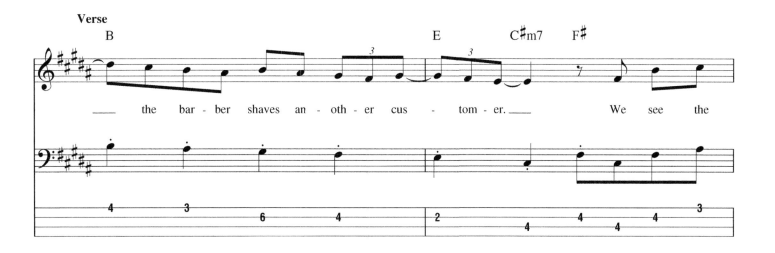

the bar - ber shaves an - oth - er cus - tom - er. ___ We see the

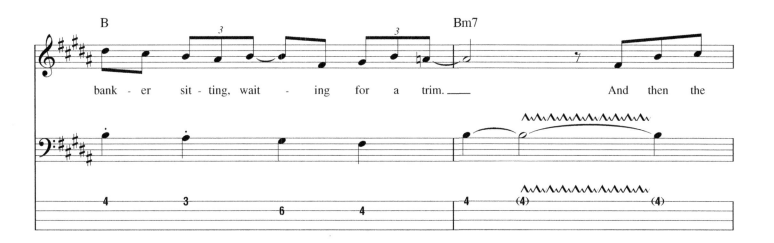

bank - er sit - ting, wait - ing for a trim. ___ And then the

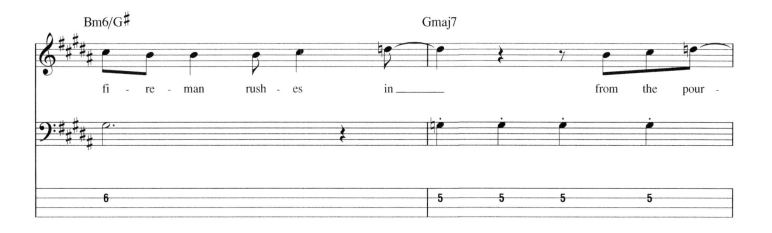

fi - re - man rush - es in ___ from the pour -

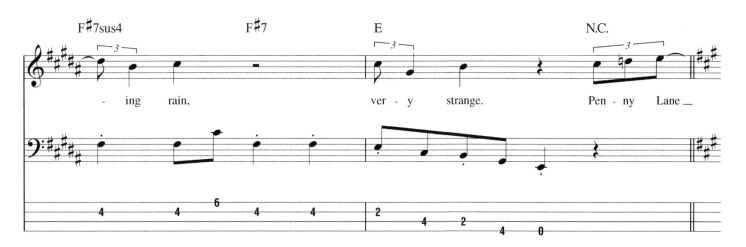

- ing rain, ver - y strange. Pen - ny Lane ___

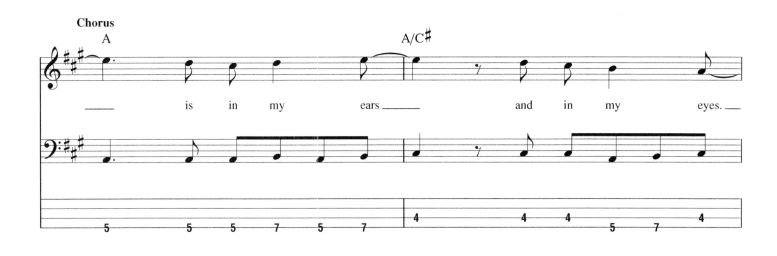

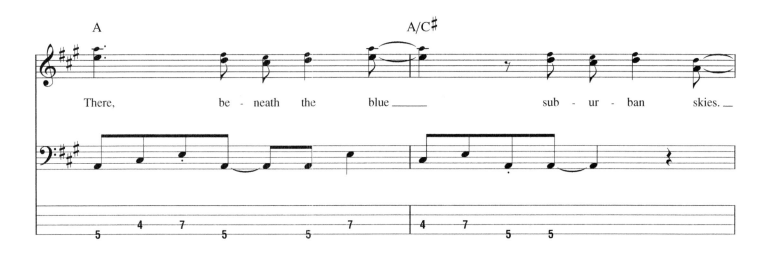

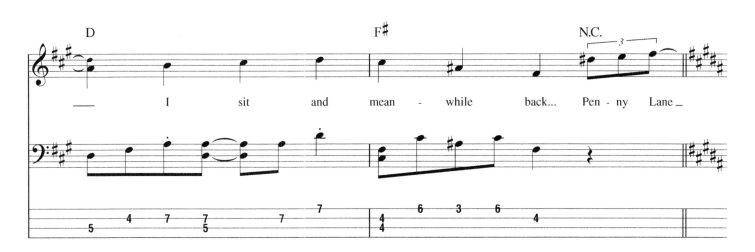

Rain

Words and Music by John Lennon and Paul McCartney

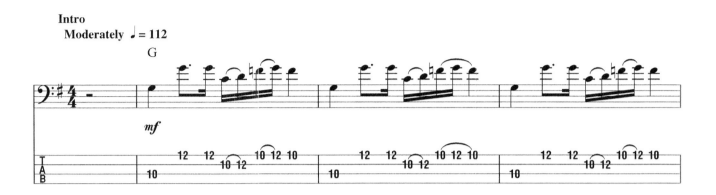

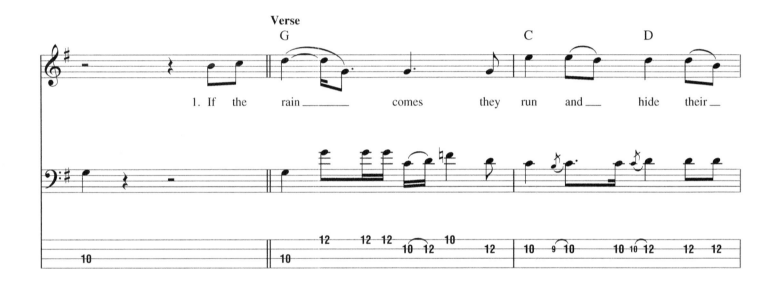

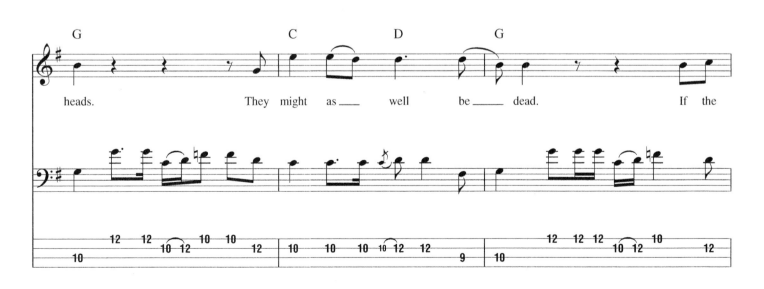

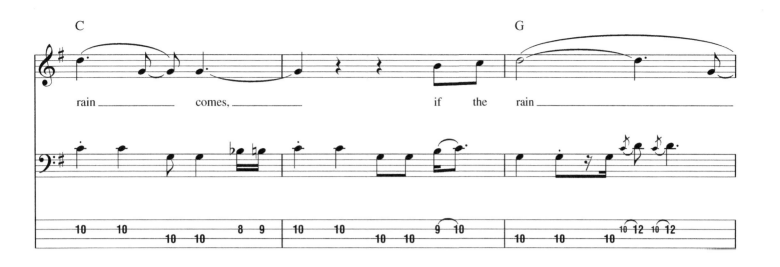

rain _____ comes, _____ if the rain _____

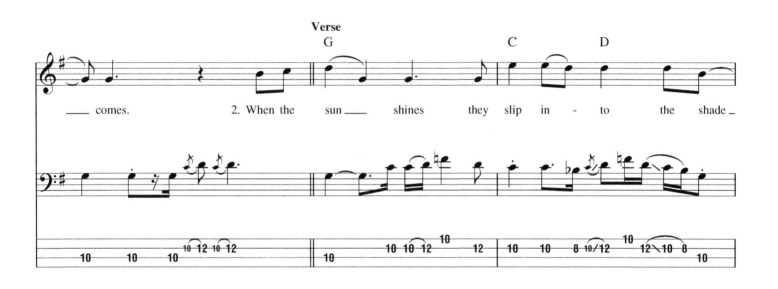

Verse

_____ comes. 2. When the sun _____ shines they slip in-to the shade _

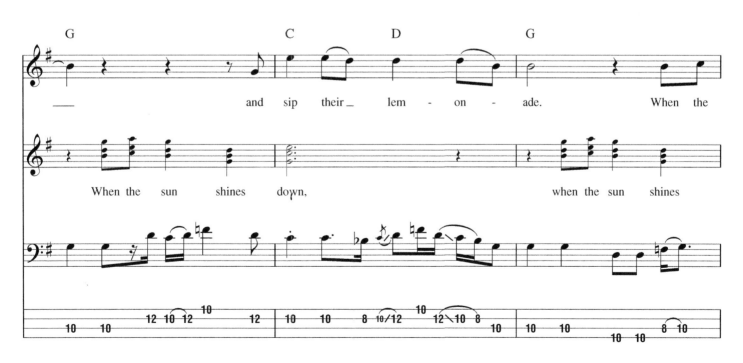

_____ and sip their _ lem - on - ade. When the

When the sun shines down, when the sun shines

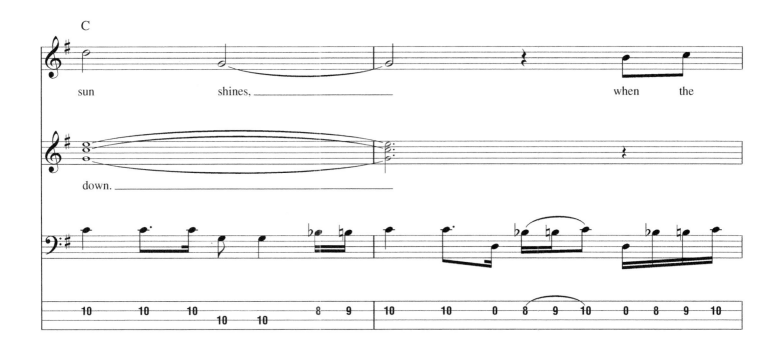

sun   shines,_____   when   the

down._____

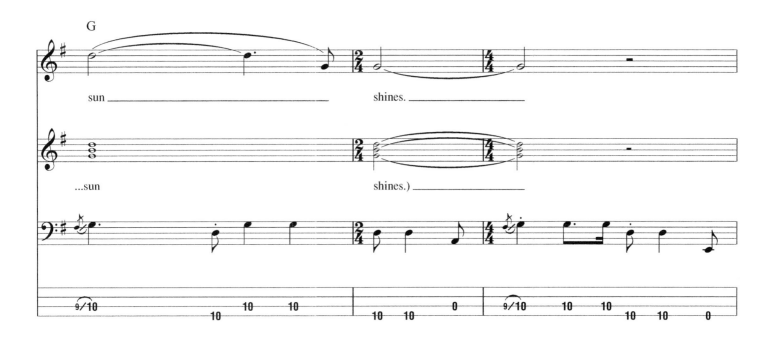

sun _____   shines._____

...sun   shines.)_____

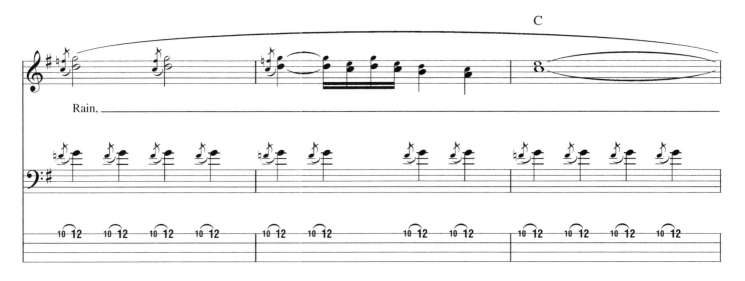

Rain,_____

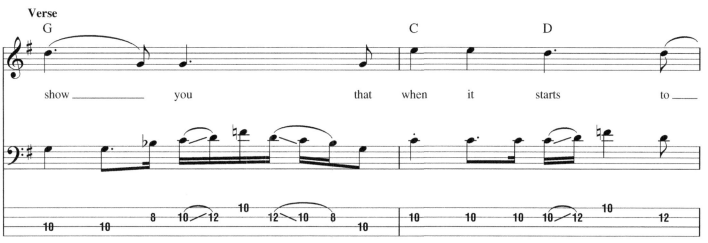

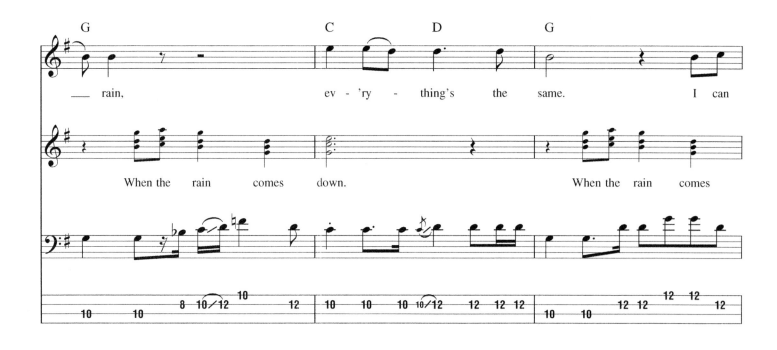

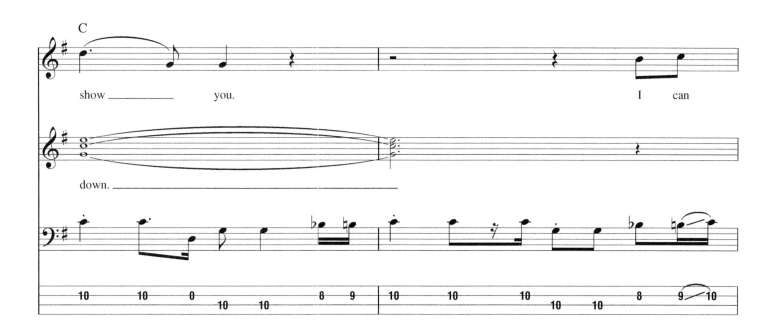

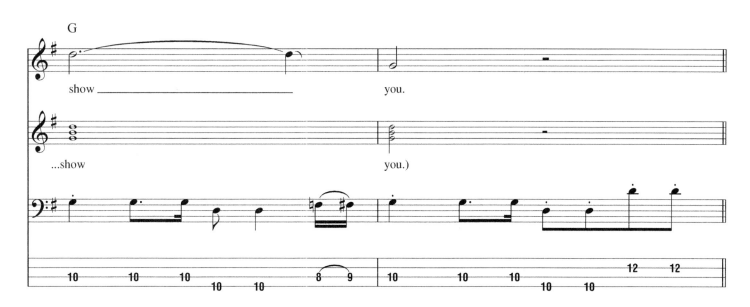

Chorus

Rain,_____
(Rain.)_____

_____ I don't mind._____

Rain,_____
(Rain.)_____

_____ the weath-er's fine._____ 4. Can you

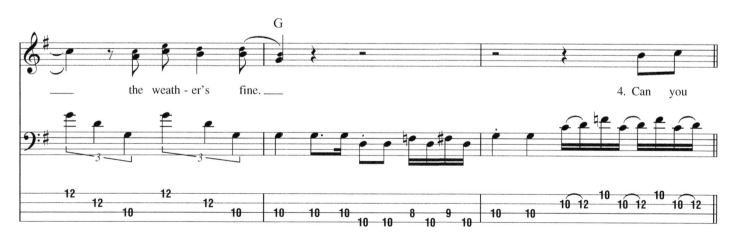

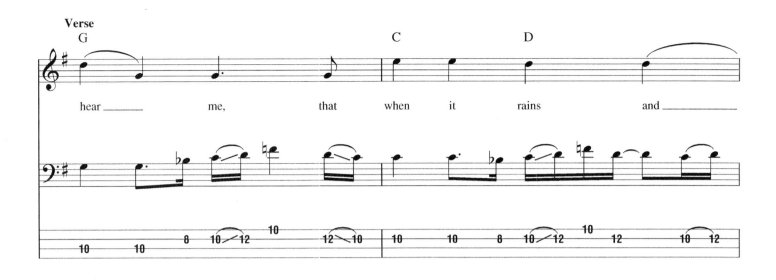

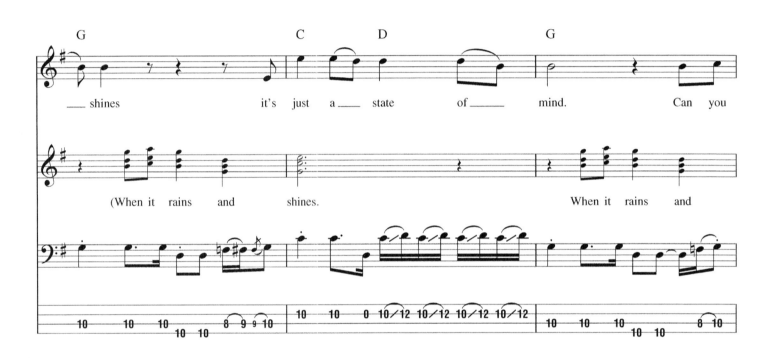

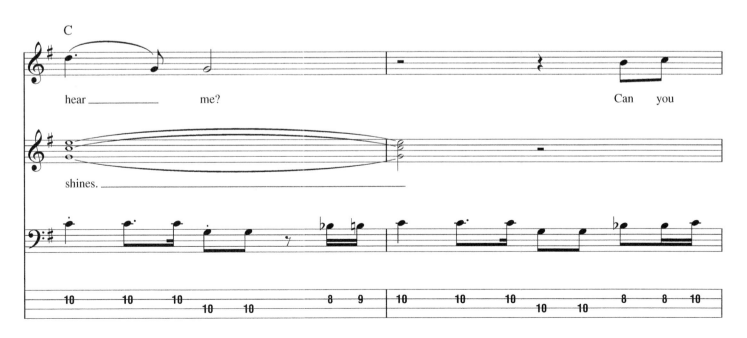

hear _____ me?

...hear   me?)

Outro
G

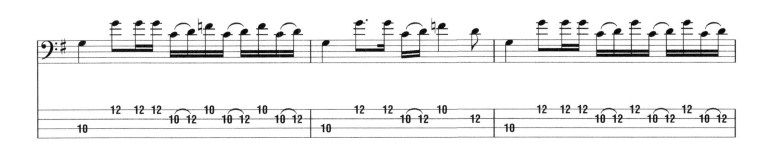

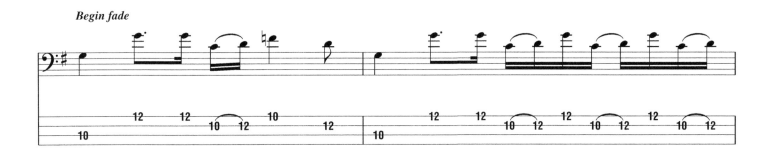

Begin fade

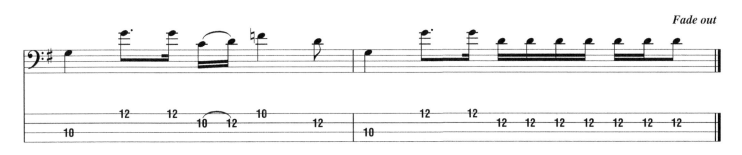

Fade out

With a Little Help from My Friends

Words and Music by John Lennon and Paul McCartney

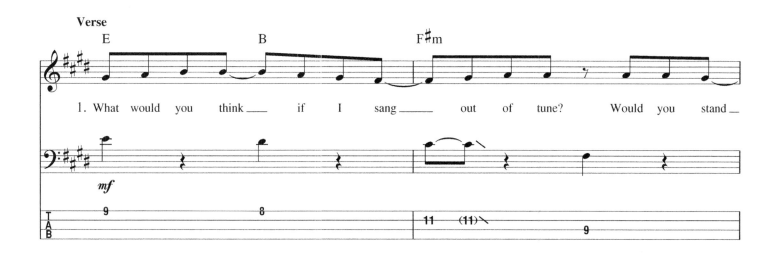

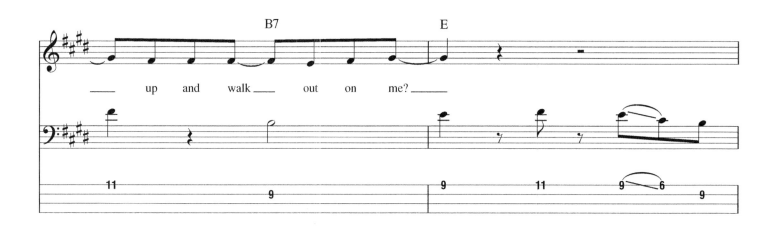

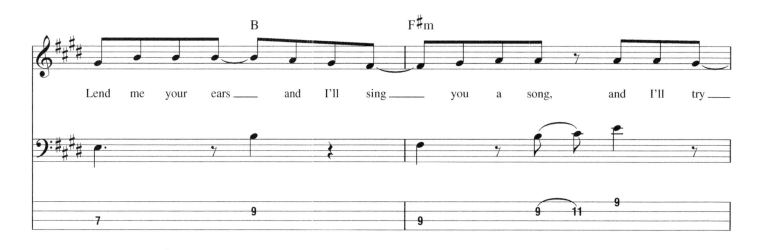

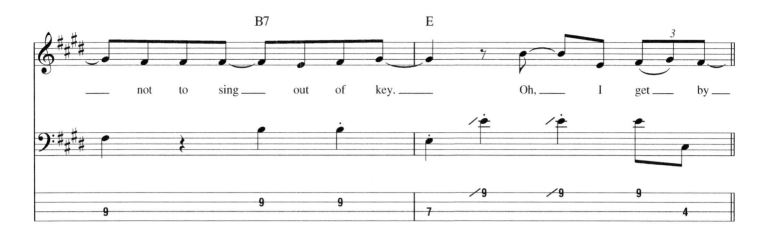

not to sing ___ out of key. ___ Oh, ___ I get ___ by ___

Chorus

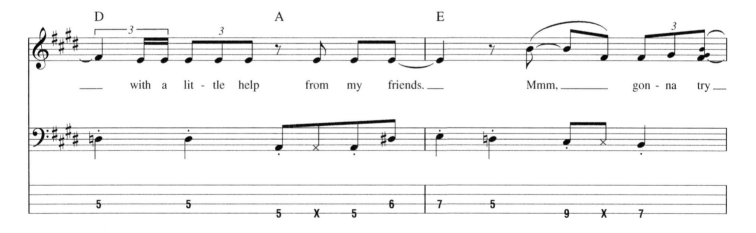

___ with a lit - tle help from my friends. ___ Mmm, ___ I get high ___

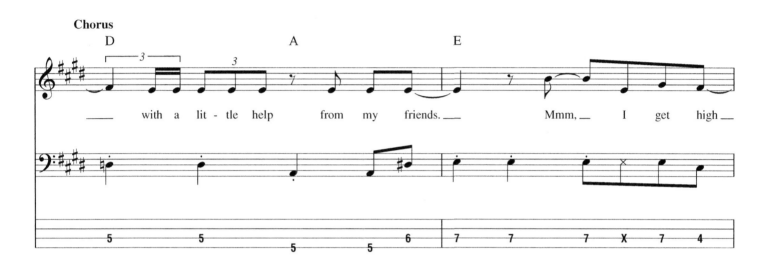

___ with a lit - tle help from my friends. ___ Mmm, ___ gon - na try ___

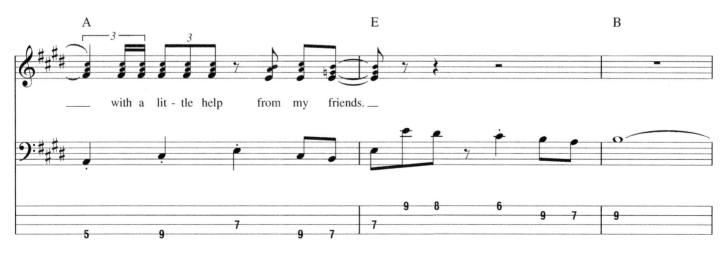

___ with a lit - tle help from my friends. ___

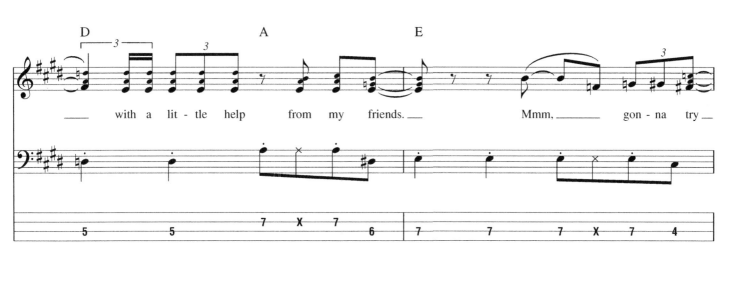

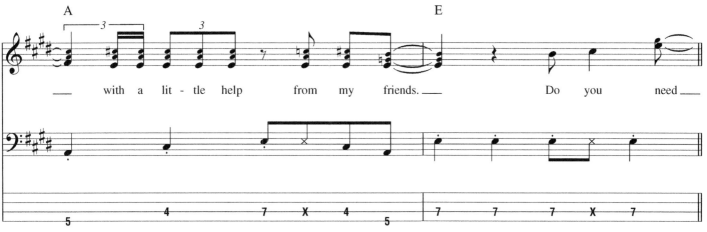

Bridge

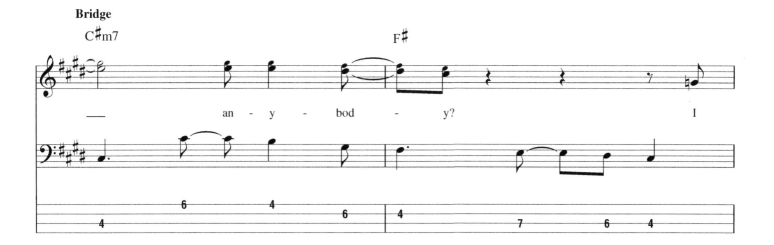

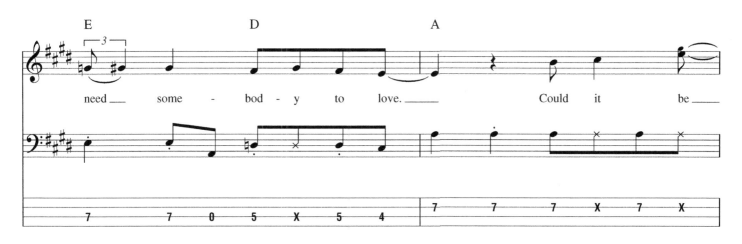

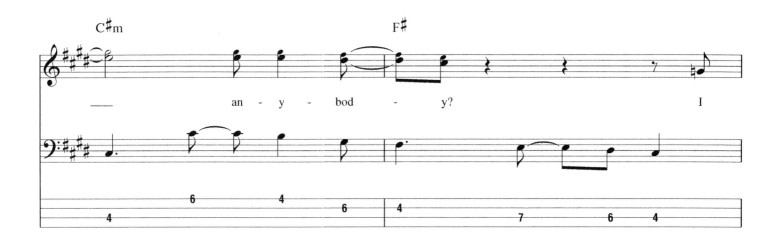

an - y - bod - y?   I

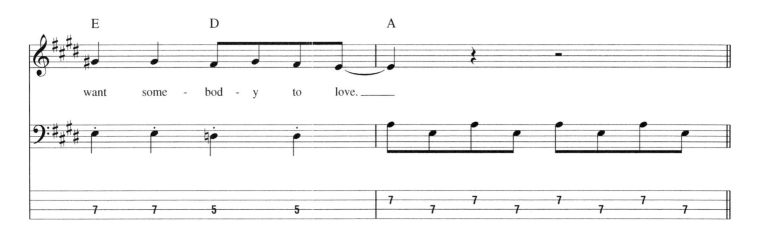

want   some - bod - y   to   love._____

Verse

3. (Would   you   be - lieve____   in   a   love____   at   first   sight?

Yes, I'm cer -

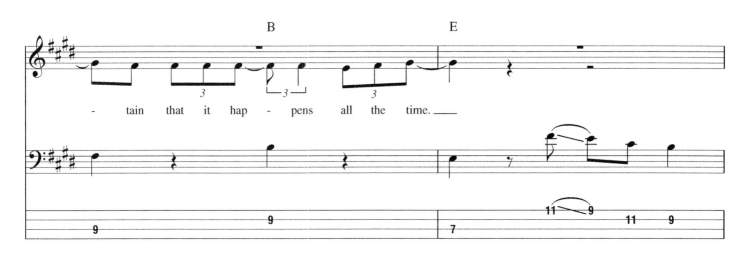

- tain   that   it   hap - pens   all   the   time._____

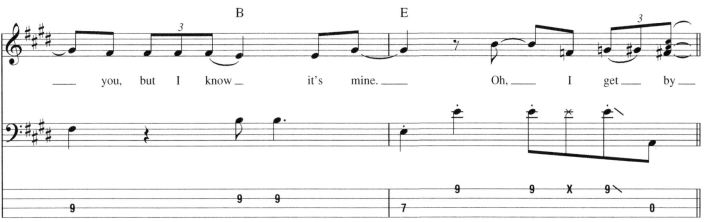

Chorus

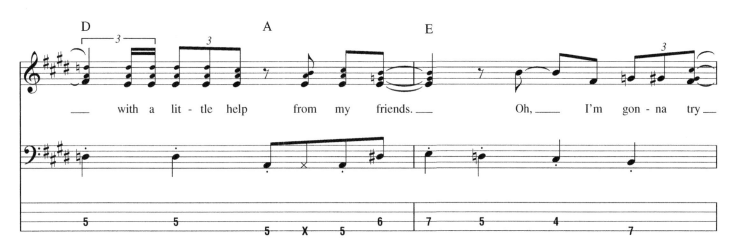

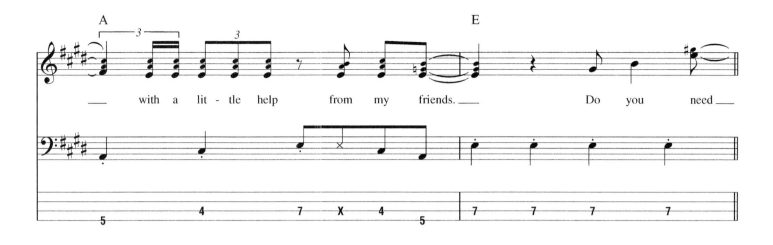

with a lit-tle help from my friends. Do you need

Bridge

an - y - bod - y? I just need some-one to

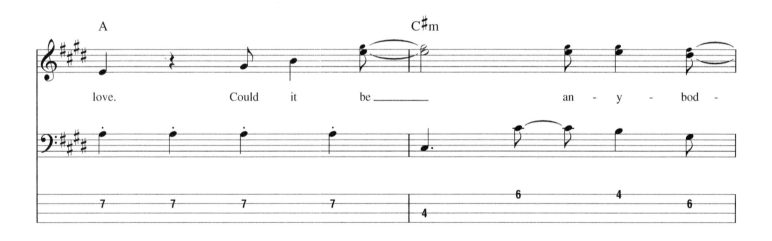

love. Could it be an - y - bod -

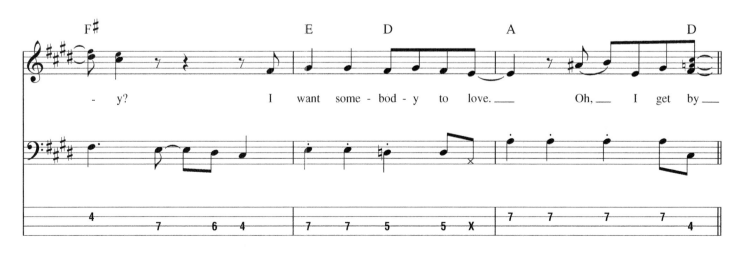

- y? I want some-bod-y to love. Oh, I get by

Silly Love Songs

Words and Music by Paul McCartney and Linda McCartney

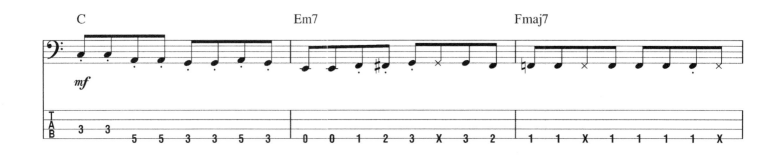

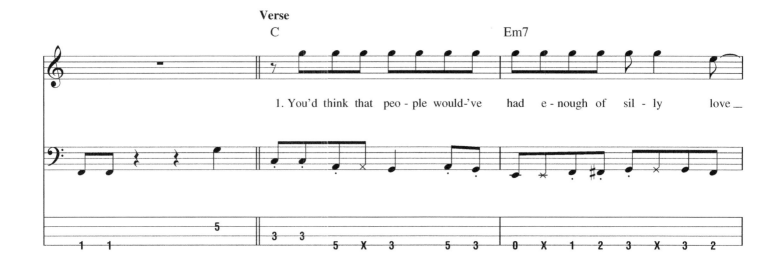

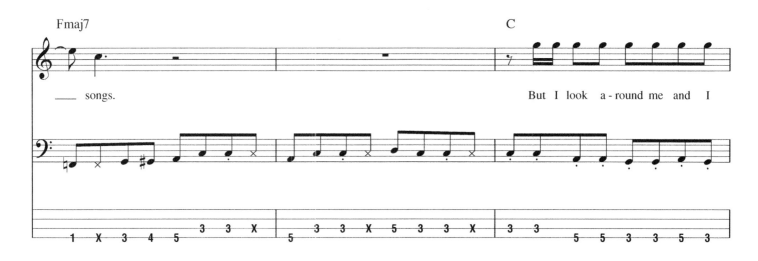

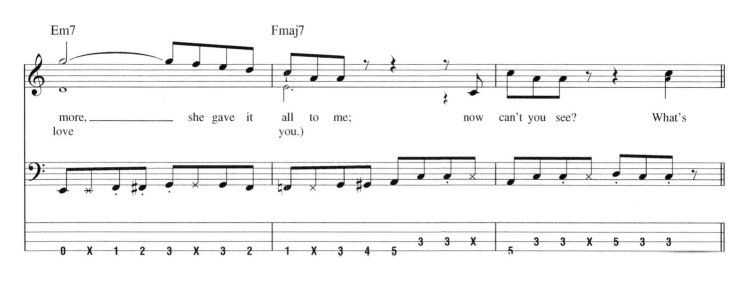

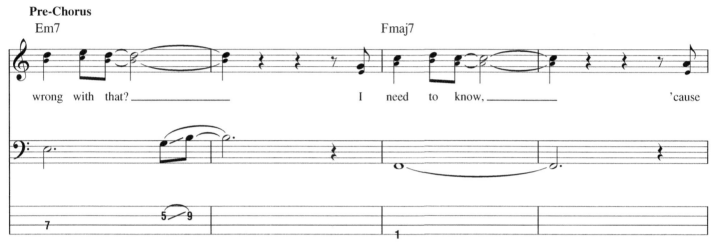

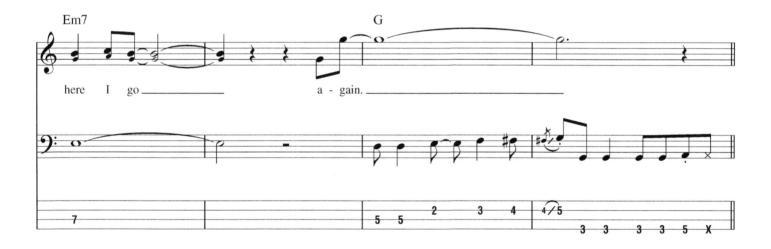

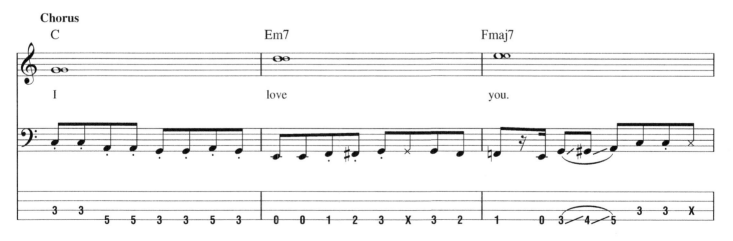

you a - bout my loved one?
you.)

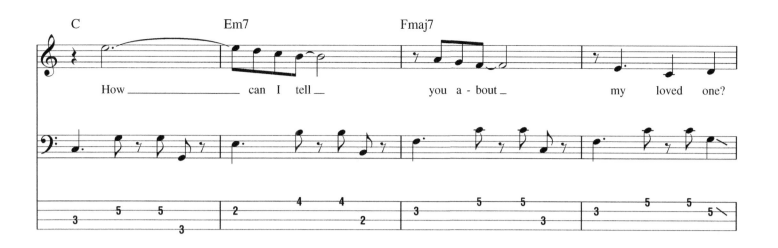

How _____ can I tell _ you a - bout _ my loved one?

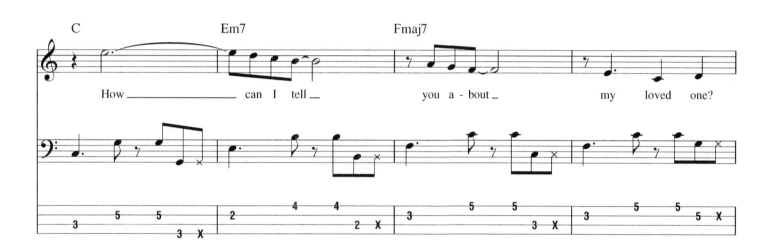

How _____ can I tell _ you a - bout _ my loved one?

How _____ can I tell _ you a - bout _ my loved one?

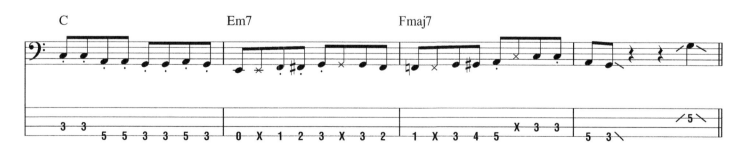

BASS RECORDED VERSIONS

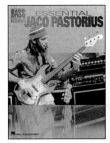
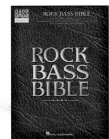

Bass Recorded Versions feature authentic transcriptions written in standard notation and tablature for bass guitar. This series features complete bass lines from the classics to contemporary superstars.

25 Essential Rock Bass Classics
00690210 / $19.99

Avenged Sevenfold – Nightmare
00691054 / $19.99

The Beatles – Abbey Road
00128336 / $24.99

The Beatles – 1962-1966
00690556 / $19.99

The Beatles – 1967-1970
00690557 / $24.99

Best of Bass Tab
00141806 / $17.99

The Best of Blink 182
00690549 / $18.99

Blues Bass Classics
00690291 / $22.99

Boston – Bass Collection
00690935 / $19.95

Stanley Clarke – Collection
00672307 / $22.99

Dream Theater – Bass Anthology
00119345 / $29.99

Funk Bass Bible
00690744 / $27.99

Hard Rock Bass Bible
00690746 / $22.99

Jimi Hendrix – Are You Experienced?
00690371 / $17.95

Jimi Hendrix – Bass Tab Collection
00160505 / $24.99

Iron Maiden – Bass Anthology
00690867 / $24.99

Jazz Bass Classics
00102070 / $19.99

The Best of Kiss
00690080 / $22.99

Lynyrd Skynyrd – All-Time Greatest Hits
00690956 / $24.99

Bob Marley – Bass Collection
00690568 / $24.99

Mastodon – Crack the Skye
00691007 / $19.99

Megadeth – Bass Anthology
00691191 / $22.99

Metal Bass Tabs
00103358 / $22.99

Best of Marcus Miller
00690811 / $29.99

Motown Bass Classics
00690253 / $19.99

Muse – Bass Tab Collection
00123275 / $22.99

Nirvana – Bass Collection
00690066 / $19.99

Nothing More – Guitar & Bass Collection
00265439 / $24.99

The Offspring – Greatest Hits
00690809 / $17.95

The Essential Jaco Pastorius
00690420 / $22.99

Jaco Pastorius – Greatest Jazz Fusion Bass Player
00690421 / $24.99

Pearl Jam – Ten
00694882 / $22.99

Pink Floyd – Dark Side of the Moon
00660172 / $19.99

The Best of Police
00660207 / $24.99

Pop/Rock Bass Bible
00690747 / $24.99

Queen – The Bass Collection
00690065 / $22.99

R&B Bass Bible
00690745 / $24.99

Rage Against the Machine
00690248 / $22.99

Red Hot Chili Peppers – BloodSugarSexMagik
00690064 / $22.99

Red Hot Chili Peppers – By the Way
00690585 / $24.99

Red Hot Chili Peppers – Californication
00690390 / $22.99

Red Hot Chili Peppers – Greatest Hits
00690675 / $22.99

Red Hot Chili Peppers – I'm with You
00691167 / $22.99

Red Hot Chili Peppers – One Hot Minute
00690091 / $22.99

Red Hot Chili Peppers – Stadium Arcadium
00690853 / Book Only $24.95

Rock Bass Bible
00690446 / $22.99

Rolling Stones – Bass Collection
00690256 / $24.99

Royal Blood
00151826 / $24.99

Rush – The Spirit of Radio: Greatest Hits 1974-1987
00323856 / $24.99

Best of Billy Sheehan
00173972 / $24.99

Slap Bass Bible
00159716 / $29.99

Sly & The Family Stone for Bass
00109733 / $24.99

Best of Yes
00103044 / $24.99

Best of ZZ Top for Bass
00691069 / $24.99

HAL•LEONARD®

Visit Hal Leonard Online at
www.halleonard.com

Prices, contents & availability subject to change without notice. Some products may not be available outside the U.S.A.

HAL•LEONARD® BASS PLAY-ALONG

The Bass Play-Along™ Series will help you play your favorite songs quickly and easily! Just follow the tab, listen to the audio to hear how the bass should sound, and then play-along using the separate backing tracks. The melody and lyrics are also included in the book in case you want to sing, or to simply help you follow along. The audio files are enhanced so you can adjust the recording to any tempo without changing pitch!

1. Rock
00699674 Book/Online Audio $16.99

2. R&B
00699675 Book/Online Audio $16.99

3. Songs for Beginners
00346426 Book/Online Audio $16.99

4. '90s Rock
00294992 Book/Online Audio $16.99

5. Funk
00699680 Book/Online Audio $16.99

6. Classic Rock
00699678 Book/Online Audio $17.99

8. Punk Rock
00699813 Book•CD Pack.............................$12.95

9. Blues
00699817 Book/Online Audio $16.99

10. Jimi Hendrix – Smash Hits
00699815 Book/Online Audio.......................$17.99

11. Country
00699818 Book/CD Pack.............................$12.95

12. Punk Classics
00699814 Book/CD Pack.............................$12.99

13. The Beatles
00275504 Book/Online Audio $17.99

14. Modern Rock
00699821 Book/CD Pack.............................$14.99

15. Mainstream Rock
00699822 Book/CD Pack.............................$14.99

16. '80s Metal
00699825 Book/CD Pack.............................$16.99

17. Pop Metal
00699826 Book•CD Pack.............................$14.99

18. Blues Rock
00699828 Book/CD Pack.............................$19.99

19. Steely Dan
00700203 Book/Online Audio $17.99

20. The Police
00700270 Book/Online Audio $19.99

21. Metallica: 1983-1988
00234338 Book/Online Audio $19.99

22. Metallica: 1991-2016
00234339 Book/Online Audio $19.99

23. Pink Floyd –
Dark Side of The Moon
00700847 Book/Online Audio $16.99

24. Weezer
00700960 Book/CD Pack............................. $17.99

25. Nirvana
00701047 Book/Online Audio $17.99

26. Black Sabbath
00701180 Book/Online Audio $17.99

27. Kiss
00701181 Book/Online Audio.......................$17.99

28. The Who
00701182 Book/Online Audio $19.99

29. Eric Clapton
00701183 Book/Online Audio $17.99

30. Early Rock
00701184 Book/CD Pack.............................$15.99

31. The 1970s
00701185 Book/CD Pack.............................$14.99

32. Cover Band Hits
00211598 Book/Online Audio $16.99

33. Christmas Hits
00701197 Book/CD Pack.............................$12.99

34. Easy Songs
00701480 Book/Online Audio $17.99

35. Bob Marley
00701702 Book/Online Audio $17.99

36. Aerosmith
00701886 Book/CD Pack.............................$14.99

37. Modern Worship
00701920 Book/Online Audio $19.99

38. Avenged Sevenfold
00702386 Book/CD Pack.............................$16.99

39. Queen
00702387 Book/Online Audio $17.99

40. AC/DC
14041594 Book/Online Audio $17.99

41. U2
00702582 Book/Online Audio $19.99

42. Red Hot Chili Peppers
00702991 Book/Online Audio.......................$19.99

43. Paul McCartney
00703079 Book/Online Audio $19.99

44. Megadeth
00703080 Book/CD Pack.............................$16.99

45. Slipknot
00703201 Book/CD Pack $17.99

46. Best Bass Lines Ever
00103359 Book/Online Audio.......................$19.99

47. Dream Theater
00111940 Book/Online Audio $24.99

48. James Brown
00117421 Book/CD Pack.............................$16.99

49. Eagles
00119936 Book/Online Audio $17.99

50. Jaco Pastorius
00128407 Book/Online Audio.......................$17.99

51. Stevie Ray Vaughan
00146154 Book/CD Pack.............................$16.99

52. Cream
00146159 Book/Online Audio $19.99

56. Bob Seger
00275503 Book/Online Audio $16.99

57. Iron Maiden
00278398 Book/Online Audio $17.99

58. Southern Rock
00278436 Book/Online Audio $17.99

HAL•LEONARD®

Prices, contents, and availability subject to change without notice.

Visit Hal Leonard Online at **www.halleonard.com**